DARK LIGHT

DARK LIGHT

DARK LIGHT

DARK LIGHT

DARK LIGHT

I

Be honest , unapologetically honest even if it pains you to say aloud, even if it might hurt others initially because the truth is the only way to real healing. When you face the truth courageously you will also be liberating yourself from the chains of lies you allowed yourself to live in. When you are able to free yourself, you also will start the process for others to be free as well. When you heal yourself, you heal others.

DARK LIGHT

II

Vision is not seen with the eyes but with the mind. You must see it, whatever that "IT" is for you, in your mind's eye first and then trust that it is already done. Notice I said, "Trust, that it is already done". I didn't say, "hope". I didn't say, "Have faith". I didn't say, "Believe". Those qualities are just steps along the way but are not meant to be the place where your vision ends. You must know it despite what is around you. Know it, despite your temporary circumstances. Know it, despite what people have told you or what they will tell you. It is what you know that will create your life, not what you believe.

DARK LIGHT

III

Who are you? At the depth of your core, who are you? What are your values? How do you let your light shine in this world? Do you try to dim your light, or do you try to dim the light of others? Are you afraid to shine?

A life without reflection is a life wasted. Getting to know you takes work but is incredibly rewarding. The wisest people on earth know themselves deeply and completely.

#KnowThyself

DARK LIGHT

IV

You don't have to be anything. Everything in your life is a choice. You can choose to be kind, compassionate, thoughtful, or you can choose to be indifferent, inconsiderate, selfish etc. All of it is a choice. When you can remove your self-judgment on qualities that can be perceived as bad or good, which isn't true anyway because they are just choices that you have made, then you can discover who you are and be ok with that. *#ThatIsFreedom*

If you choose to work on qualities that you no longer have a need for then they will be easier to replace because you have now figured out why you needed those qualities

DARK LIGHT

in the first place. Just be and allow yourself to be. There is liberty in knowing that you don't have to do or be anything. Then you can act genuinely and authentically from your truest self. If you choose to work on qualities that you no longer have a need for then they will be easier to replace because you have now figured out why you needed those qualities in the first place. There is liberty in knowing that you don't have to do or be anything. Then you can act genuine and authentic from your truest self. Just be and allow yourself to be.

DARK LIGHT

V

Life has a way of showing you who people are. There is a strong possibility that some people that you are close to do not have your best interests at heart. There are people who you are around that not only don't care about you but also, in fact, want to see you fail. This is a fact of life. Regardless of how well you try to treat people you will not be liked, in fact, some will even hate you. The most you can do is understand yourself and do what is best for you. You cannot change or save anyone but yourself. Only you can save you.

DARK LIGHT

VI

The only thing you have to follow is your heart. That along with your intuition will bring you where you need and want to go. Following what someone else has done can only take you so far. Ultimately, their path worked for them because it was meant for them. Your story doesn't have to look like anyone else's, and it's not meant to. That's why it lives within you. And you are the only one who can carry it out. In fact, you're the only one that is meant to.

DARK LIGHT

VII

Sometimes when observing a problem or situation, it is easy to get caught up in trying to fix the manifestations. The manifestations are only the symptoms to a deeper issue. Instead of trying to fix the symptoms, go deeper and try to fix the problem. Instead of focusing on the effect, focus on the cause. Take advantage of the opportunity that today has given you: to be fully present. It is when you are fully present, you can then see all the good that is unfolding before you. You can see all that is, and has been, just by being fully aware of the moments that lie before you. In this place, you can experience the richness of what it means to be alive, and what it means to live.

DARK LIGHT

VIII

What kind of impact do you want to have on the world? What kind of life do you want to lead and are you living it now? The type of impact you have on the world and people has nothing to do with material things. Even if you feel you have no money to give, kindness is always free. But of course this depends on what impact you want to have. I'm not talking about caring about what people think about you, no matter what, people will think what they want. But no matter how people think of you, your actions will always be a true representation of who you are. How you treat others, is the truest measure of character.

DARK LIGHT

IX

How much are you willing to work on yourself to create the life that you say you want? Your problems will go with you everywhere, even when your circumstances change. Conversely, changing the way you deal with you when situations arise, or your perception, can change the circumstance without any external factors being altered. The key to it all, is dealing, working and getting to know YOU, because ultimately, YOU have everything you need, regardless of the situation.

DARK LIGHT

X

Love is a courageous act. I don't mean love, the adjective. I am referring to love, the verb. How do you treat people with love that are filled with hate? How do you find the courage and compassion to treat those with love that would certainly not treat you with the same? How do you move through life with kindness and compassion in a world that is constructed off of ignorance, hate and racist ideologies? I certainly do not have the answers. The one thing that I do know is that change and courageous love comes from within first.

DARK LIGHT

XI

If you want to learn how to live, observe nature. Animals need things, but they never hurry to get them. Plants never need to be taught how to grow, because they just flow with the beat of life. Plants only go and grow towards Light. Many will say that life is complicated for us because we are more intelligent than every other being. While I agree we are more intelligent, I don't agree that we ACT more intelligently. All animals use intuition, and even though they have the ability to have thoughts, they KNOW that thoughts aren't always needed. They just ACT. When you just go with the flow and follow your intuition, you are using what ALL of us were born with. When you start to observe nature, it is intelligent. When you realize you are a PART of nature that is enlightenment.

DARK LIGHT

<u>XII</u>

If life is a book, you are the author. If life is a movie, you are the director, the producer and a part of the cast. You are, and the only, Master creator of your life. You can change your universe, simply by changing yourself. When you open the doors and windows to your own soul, in order to understand it and to get to know the deepest parts of you, then you are able to let in light. Light only comes in through open doors and open windows. You cannot expect to benefit from all the universe has to offer if you do not let the light in. The only way to let the light in is to open yourself up to you, to those who know others are intelligent, and those who know themselves as wise.

DARK LIGHT

XIII

There is so much going on in the world. So much we can look at, observe or be a part of. However the view of the world always depends on the viewer. You choose to focus on what's wrong or what's right.

You can choose to ignore or to embrace the wrong or right in the world. Or you can try to walk the tightrope of life embracing all you come across. One might ask, "If I am to embrace all, how do you embrace the suffering of others?" Embrace it with love and compassion and then let that manifest in any way that it might.

To love people truly, deeply, and completely

DARK LIGHT

regardless of where they are at is not only expressing love in its deepest form, but is also a courageous act.

DARK LIGHT

XIV

Sometimes when you let go of certain situations, you end up letting go of certain people. There's nothing wrong with that even if it feels bad, because sometimes we hold on to situations and to people much longer than we were supposed to. It's OK to move forward even if you feel like you're leaving someone behind. Ultimately you have to do what's best for you and you're the only one who truly knows what that is. Wish people the best and *#MoveForward*

DARK LIGHT

XV

Our situations aren't always pretty but there is always beauty to be experienced in life. Oftentimes we miss the beauty around us because we are removed from the moment. Don't look back, don't look ahead, just take in this moment, wherever you are.

#BeautyIsAllAroundUs

When you look at your situation from the ground level, it might look cloudy and dark, with no end in sight. When you start to rise above your current situation, you will not only see the light, but you'll realize it never left. Clouds and storms will come and go, but light will always remain.

DARK LIGHT

XVI

It is amazing what you can observe in silence. If you are around a lot of people at any given time, take a moment to just watch. Try not to judge, because your judgment will take you out of the moment and will obstruct your observations. Simply watch. Quiet the internal dialogue and focus on watching and you'll be surprised at what you learn about them, and about you.

Acknowledge your fears, get to know them and embrace them. The mistake people make is that many are unwilling to move forward with action because their fear has not been alleviated or has not dissipated.

DARK LIGHT

XVII

Bring it with you on the journey. Think of it this way, **#FEAR** is like a tank of water with no lid and book-bag straps for you to carry on your back.

As you go through whatever you're doing, water (aka fear) is constantly spilling out. Therefore the more you do, the more water spills out. Eventually, you'll be so engrossed in your actions that you'll realize there's no more water (fear) left.

#IfYouDoNotKnowFear

#HowWillYouBecomeFearless?

DARK LIGHT

XVIII

We will not always get what we want, but we certainly get what we need more often than not. Getting what you need may not be preferred, but obviously there is something about what you're getting that is necessary, otherwise you would not be receiving it. Until you learn the lesson about whatever it is you're getting, or until you realize that on some level you know you need it too, you'll keep getting what you are getting.

#GettingTheLessonWillGetYouWhatYouWant

#GetIt?

DARK LIGHT

XIX

Sometimes all you can do is throw your hands up in the air and say thank you. If you have given it your best, if the situation is out of your control, then all you can do is be thankful that you woke up to experience it.

#BeThankful for the lesson.

#BeThankful for the life.

#BeThankful for the people in your life and

#BeThankful for the people who are not.

#BeThankful for your health.

 #BeThankful for where you are at and where you are going. When you focus on the good things it shifts your attention and focus and then you can attract more of what you want, and less of what you don't. And if

DARK LIGHT

the situation is out of control anyway, why are you wasting your energy focusing on it?

DARK LIGHT

XX

You were born to be successful. You were born to be great. You were born to strive because you were born with a purpose. You don't need to wonder what your purpose is, because it hasn't gone anywhere, it hasn't changed. You just need to remember. Remember what you loved to do before friends, family and society told you that you couldn't make money doing that? Remember what you loved to do before people uttered words of what you "can't", "couldn't" and "shouldn't do? Remember what you Loved before you believed the Lies? You have all the answers for your life within you. Just have the courage to listen and follow. # *BeAFaithfulServantToYou*

DARK LIGHT

XXI

If you learn to love yourself, fully and unconditionally, then you will realize what true love looks like. You will be more open to receiving unconditional love if you already unconditionally love yourself. Unfortunately, the fact is, if you don't unconditionally love yourself then why would anyone else?

DARK LIGHT

XXII

Your dreams are yours and oftentimes yours alone. Sometimes your dreams need protecting from the negative energy other people give. This is not to say that they are all "hating" (though some are) but sometimes people have a hard time stepping out of their own small box, therefore it would be extremely difficult for them to understand why you are out of yours. Send them love and peace, even if they don't send it back, because that same love and peace will come back to you anyway.

#ProtectYourDreams #LifeLessons

DARK LIGHT

XXIII

Forgive, forgive, and forgive. You may think forgiveness is about the other person but that is far from the truth. The other person doesn't suffer because you're holding on to what they did; only you do. Forgiveness is about you. For those among my friends who are more religious here's another point; you can't be unforgiving to others and expect the God that you worship to forgive you.

#LifeLessons

DARK LIGHT

XXIV

We so often use a facade to mask suffering. So often people look like they are well when they are really troubled. This is why it is so important to be kind to people, no matter what vibes they give off, no matter how much you may not even want to be around them. Kindness heals. You, unfortunately, cannot save anyone but yourself. However, you can be kind to everyone.

#KindnessHeals

DARK LIGHT

XXV

Life speaks to us in so many ways, the question is, are you listening? Even if you didn't pay attention to the little voice inside of you, there are so many other ways in which life is giving you the lesson you need. Pay attention. Repeated circumstances are not about the other party, they are about you. If you learned your lesson before, then you wouldn't be repeating the class. *#LifeLessons #LifeHints #WakeUp*

DARK LIGHT

XXVI

I had a conversation with a girl about makeup today at a sleep away summer camp. The camp rules specify that you may not wear makeup while working. Anyway, she said that she is dying for her day off so that she can put on makeup again. Ultimately, she felt bad about herself without it. She asked me if it was weird, I told her no, but it was unfortunate. It was unfortunate because she felt as though she needed it to go out in the world and not feel badly about herself.

No one should ever feel they need something external, to make them feel good about the internal. When you genuinely feel

DARK LIGHT

good about the internal, anything else you add is an addition, not a necessity.

#lovetheInternal

DARK LIGHT

<u>**XXVII**</u>

Sometimes we mess up. And sometimes it's in a really big way. We make mistakes with our parents, friends, significant others, our co-workers and our bosses. After you do all you can to make amends let it go. There is no point wasting energy wallowing in the past and beating yourself up for it. Reflect; make sure you don't make the same mistake twice. Let it go!

DARK LIGHT

XXVIII

Be. Just be. Don't daydream about the future and don't wallow in the past. Just be in this moment and embrace it while it's here. Even if it were uncomfortable, even if it's a situation you'd rather not be in. If you fully embrace the present, you'll gain insight and wisdom that you would have missed if you were mentally somewhere else. Be in the present fully, so you don't miss all the lessons and wisdom that can be attained. After all, technically, the present is all you ever have.

DARK LIGHT

XXIX

The true measure of someone's character is not by how they treat their friends, or people that they know. Anyone who has a heart can treat people well. The true measure of a person's character is how they treat people that don't like them.

How do you treat people who have the intention, consciously or unconsciously, for you to fail? How do you treat those who want to see them suffer? How do you treat those that hate you? That is the true mark of a person's integrity.

DARK LIGHT

XXX

To live a peaceful life, one must realize and accept that everything changes. Nothing is constant, nothing lasts forever and the more you can accept and adapt to change, the more peaceful life you will have.

DARK LIGHT

XXXI

I went through a quick series of emotions today at the Macy's store. An employee followed me around the store seemingly waiting for me to steal something. From curiosity, to surprise, to annoyed, to anger, to sadness, to eventually peace.

The peace came because gradually I had the clarity of mind to realize that those conscious and unconscious bigoted beliefs have nothing to do with me. Realize that more often than not, someone's unjustified bigotry, resentment, or anger has nothing to do with you. When you can see that, realize, and embrace that then serenity will follow.

DARK LIGHT

XXXII

In this moment, wherever you are, is exactly where you need to be, because if you didn't you wouldn't be there. The key is, tuning in fully to where you are; otherwise you miss many opportunities, when you are not fully engaged in the moment. When you are fully engaged in the process, and not the results, you will learn about not only the circumstances you are in, but also you will learn about yourself. All knowledge is self-knowledge but to learn about self you have to be tuned in.

#TuneInToYou

DARK LIGHT

XXXIII

It has been a long year. You have grown and learned a lot. You may have lost some people, and possibly gained some people in your life. Ultimately, finding yourself is the greatest gift that anyone can have. I have learned and continue to learn to let go, to live in the moment, and be grateful for who and what is in my life, because everything and everyone can teach you a lesson. I wish for joy, peace and love to reign in all of your lives, and for you to live out your purpose and know your worth.

#BeGreatThanBecomeGreater

#LetYourLightShine #HappyNewYear

DARK LIGHT

XXXIV

In order to create a more humane, caring, compassionate society, we need to start incorporating what Dr. Martin Luther King called a "dangerous selflessness", which means possibly putting yourself at risk to help another person who needs it. The thought process behind this philosophy is simple: In every situation instead of thinking "what will happen to me if I do this for them?" think "what would happen to them if I don't?"

#Life #DangerousSelflessness

DARK LIGHT

XXXV

Life is about letting in and letting go. It's about breathing in and breathing out. It's about being in the moment, while remembering the past and envisioning a better future. It's about going for what you want, without being attached to the results. It's about planting seeds and watching them grow. It's about learning about yourself, so you can better understand everyone else. Life is complex, not complicated, unless you make it so.

DARK LIGHT

XXXVI

Who are you? We may respond to that by stating our name, or occupation or whatever we align ourselves with. But even when we get down to the characteristics of ourselves that still doesn't really answer the question. The question looks for an answer of how you define yourself. Defy definition! Thinking outside of the box is easy once you realize that you're the one that creates the box.

DARK LIGHT

XXXVII

Listening is more important than talking. If you listen well enough, you'll be able to respond appropriately. Listening also is required internally. Listening to yourself is the voice of intuition, so listen carefully. The wisdom inside will help you survive outside. Love, light and prosperity!

DARK LIGHT

XXXVIII

There will always be things/situations that are out of your control. Worrying about them will not do any good but this is common knowledge. So how do you not worry? By letting go. Letting go doesn't mean you don't care about the thing/circumstance or person anymore, it just simply means that you are choosing to let actions take their course and realizing that you can only affect what is in your control.

DARK LIGHT

Life is meant to be simple. Even if it is a great task or a lofty goal, working on it, little by little, you will be able to attain it. Working on something "little by little" eventually you'll only have "a little" left. Rushing may leave you burnt out. Always remember, " Slow and steady wins the race." If you are a parent, teacher, or other person entrusted to lead the youth, remember this; Children will only do what you do, and not do what you say, if you don't DO what YOU say.

DARK LIGHT

XL

You have the power to act; you do not have the power to influence the result. Therefore, you must "act without the anticipation of the result, without succumbing to inaction." -The Bhagavad-Gita. Stress can only be alleviated when we emotionally detach ourselves from the result. Act without expecting.

DARK LIGHT

XLI

So a woman said to me yesterday, "When New Year's comes around, I'm going to change a lot of things about myself and be a better person." My response was, "why are you waiting until New Years?" You can start your New Year right now. The only thing we have is the present. Do what you can change and let go of what you can't.

DARK LIGHT

XLII

Kindness is not something that should be acted every once in a while. It is something that we should feel as well as act upon everyday. We need to be kind to others, as well as to ourselves. This kindness to ourselves includes mental, emotional, physical and spiritual well-being. If you're not being good to yourself, today, ask yourself, why not?

DARK LIGHT

XLIII

We tend to get what we expect, so if you expect negative things, it will come, and the same goes for positive things. Choosing to expect nothing sometimes is best, but if we are going to expect anything, expect things that will lift you up, not bring you down.

DARK LIGHT

XLIV

Take time to notice the small things, for it is because of the little things that make the big things matter. Acknowledge the small, and you will be able to appreciate the large. Every tree starts out as a seed.

DARK LIGHT

Think of your path to fulfillment like a book bag; only when it is empty, is when it has the possibility to be filled. If your mind is filled with other things that don't matter, how do you expect to attain what does matter? If you want to know what you are supposed to do in life, be still like a pond, because only still water reveals a reflection.

DARK LIGHT

XLVI

Today, can be the day, where you decide to change for the better. Right in this moment, can be the time where decide that you want more out of life, and you can make steps towards that goal. The present is all we have to become whomever we want to be in this life. Be thankful for each and every day and moment and make the most out of it.

DARK LIGHT

XLVII

Never wait for a "national" day to celebrate something when you can celebrate it everyday. It doesn't have to take the meaning completely out of the day; it just means that the nature of the holiday permeates throughout your life, not just on that day. Celebrate love, thankfulness, and gratitude, everyday.

DARK LIGHT

XLVIII

Remember this question; "Do you see the glass as 1/2 empty or 1/2 full?" Why do you have to see the glass as either? Why can't it just be 1/2, with the possibility of it being equally close to full and to empty? You don't have to be confined to choices presented by others, because even within those, we can create our own. Think critically, and creatively and you will be rewarded.

DARK LIGHT

XLIX

In life, you are the architect, the designer, the interior decorator, and the occupant. Therefore you can create something you would love to live in, or a living hell. You have all the tools, and your life will be a result of how you use them.

DARK LIGHT

L

Life is like a ride; there is no need for explanation, only a need for occupants. There is no need to rush because the final destination would mean the end of the ride. Just enjoy it, try to steer in a direction you feel you should go in, but don't be opposed to going in a different one. A different road may also lead you to where you want to be.

DARK LIGHT

LI

Someone is always watching. I'm not talking about conspiracy theory here, but literally someone is always watching. There are many people who preach what they say they practice, but they don't practice what they preach. It would be better to say not much and then do more, rather than say a lot and do very little. After all, someone is always watching. Happiness is a habit, unfortunately, so is sadness.

DARK LIGHT

LII

Your life can be meaningful, full of substance and love, or it can be empty and superficial. It IS your choice. You can choose to be a victim of circumstance, or you can allow that circumstance to mold you into a person who can be an inspiration to others. Remember "what obstacles lie around you and in front of you are only small matters compared to what lies within you." -Ralph Waldo Emerson

DARK LIGHT

LIII

Want to remember your passion? Ask yourself "What would I do for free?" What would you do, and wouldn't need to get paid to do it? If you say," nothing" you're deceiving yourself because technically you do things for free all the time. This process of self-inquiry will tap into what has never left, your purpose.

DARK LIGHT

LIV

It's never too late to try something new, to pick up where you left off, or to be the person you want to be. We have created this idea that only in certain parts of our life we can do or become certain things. This is only true if you believe it. Choose to say, "this is the day where I can create the person I want to be, do the things that I've always wanted to do and live the way I want to live.

DARK LIGHT

LV

The key to networking is for it not to be
superficial. Seek to make genuine relationships
with people. Don't do it just because they have
something you can gain from. Do it because
you'll make the relationship mutually
beneficial; what can you do for them? Even if
you don't know for sure, that still doesn't mean
you don't have something to offer, even if it's
just friendship. Be authentic, be honest, and be
yourself.

DARK LIGHT

LVI

In order to become all that you feel you want to be, discipline is a Must. If you are truly in touch with yourself, then discipline becomes easy. It is only when we are not truly in tune with ourselves that we find ourselves tempted to do things that would hinder where we want to go. To be in touch with yourself is to love yourself enough, to not get in your own way, or figure out why you are doing it.

DARK LIGHT

LVII

3 questions that need to be asked of yourself; Where are you going, Is it leading to where you said you wanted to go, and if not, are you willing to change directions? Answer honestly because these questions only help if you are being true to yourself. Sometimes the hardest conversations to have are the ones that are internal.

DARK LIGHT

LVIII

I question you to ask yourself the same question the caterpillar asked Alice, 'Who Are You?' That single question may take a lifetime to truly figure out. However, the process is much more rewarding than living without ever truly knowing who you are. Ask with intention, honesty, serenity, and love will be waiting there at the very core of your existence.

DARK LIGHT

LIX

Hope as well as Fear by themselves, are empty. It is only Faith that gives these things substance. Faith is when there is a belief connected to either one of these feelings. You can choose what you want to have faith in, and that, will always lead you where you need to be. When you are able to let go of everything, anything is possible. Move in the direction you want, without being emotionally tied to the outcome. Be open.

DARK LIGHT

LX

Challenge yourself to think critically about your life individually, and your life within the world around us. It is not enough to simply allow yourself to become indifferent to injustice. Even if you were not out protesting, at least having a meaningful conversation about the world around us, would be a start.

.

DARK LIGHT

LXI

Now although happiness comes from within, the people you surround yourself with also encourage it. In many ways, you are, who your friends are. If there weren't strong commonalities, then they wouldn't be your friends. Examine the differences and similarities of your friends and compare them to you. You may learn a lot more than you asked for.

DARK LIGHT

LXII

All happiness and joy are choices that we choose to make. Even if you are not content with where you are at, it doesn't mean you can't be happy. When you choose to embrace positive feelings, positive manifestations will arise.

DARK LIGHT

LXIII

Often times we know what to do, we just don't do it. How bad do you want the life that you say you want? How willing are you to make sacrifices to get to what you want? Are you flexible in your thinking to attain your goal? If you're not asking yourself these questions, why haven't you?

DARK LIGHT

LXIV

It is important to pursue our own ventures that interest us, although it is just as important to pursue ventures bigger than ourselves. There are people/causes, which need not only your attention, or your money, but also your time. Life rewards those who are willing to give. Give more, and you will receive more, but certainly don't give with the sole purpose of receiving.

.

DARK LIGHT

LXV

Often times we are looking for the bigger things in life and we miss the smaller things, we look for the extravagant and miss the simple. Life is made to be simple; we make it difficult. Take delight and appreciate the smaller things in life, often times, they are what's really important. It's hard to fix anything if you're caught up within the problem. Take some time to step back from it to examine and find a solution, or accept whatever it is, and things becomes easier.

DARK LIGHT

LXVI

Sometimes we make statements in life like, "I was raised to do it this way" or "I was brought up thinking this way". Just because you learned something one way, doesn't mean that's the only way it can be done. And if you don't like the way you were brought up doing something, there is no time like the present to RE -raise yourself. What can be learned, can be unlearned, the 1st step is belief.

DARK LIGHT

LXVII

Sometimes we get so caught up in what we wish we could have, that we minimize what we actually have. There is nothing wrong in wanting more, but there is something wrong in not appreciating what you have already received. Rule of thumb: If you're not grateful for what you have, you won't be grateful for what you get.

DARK LIGHT

LXVIII

Acknowledgment is the first step towards progress. You can't go in a different direction if you don't acknowledge the direction you're going in first. If you want to "get over" something, first admit that you're not over it. Acknowledgment isn't the only step towards improvement, but without it, moving forward becomes much more difficult.

DARK LIGHT

LXIX

When we start to discover our roads of life internally, external roads become much easier to follow. The journey inward will help the journey outward. None are wiser than those who have mastered themselves. May the light shine on you, and within you, all the days of your life.

.

DARK LIGHT

LXX

Sometimes it feels wonderful to get caught up in "entertainment news", but this can be a wasteful use of time if it is not done in moderation. People like to watch and get lost in the lives of other people, but why don't you make YOUR life more entertaining? If the people that are on TV now, spent their lives watching other people, they wouldn't be on TV. Instead of living through others, live through you!

DARK LIGHT

LXXI

Although we seek direct answers to questions, many questions have no direct answer. This is why our lives should not just be rooted in facts and theories and concepts but should be lived intuitively. True wisdom and answers for your life, comes from within.

DARK LIGHT

LXXII

It's not just about what you say to other people, it's also about what you say to yourself. "I'm lazy", "I'm not good at ____," "I don't read". Really, what you're telling yourself is, "I am not willing to get better or work on those things. That is the time when people accept behaviors as a part of their character. These are all habits that can be changed whenever we want. Something you're "not good at" may just be underdeveloped.

DARK LIGHT

LXXIII

Honor yourself and love yourself enough to know that being true to you is the highest priority. With this, you will also be true to others. If you can't be honest with yourself, how honest can you be with others?

DARK LIGHT

LXXIV

Go forth in whatever you desire, without expectation. The stress that we incur sometimes is because things aren't going the way we want them to go. But this doesn't mean they are going towards what we want. Be open and be able to adjust to situations intuitively. Keep your mind open as the sky, and as clear as a glass of water.

DARK LIGHT

LXXV

It doesn't matter how wise you are, how true your words are, they cannot be forced onto anyone. Even when your intentions are good, and even if the other person knows your intention, they will only listen to you when they are ready. Wisdom cannot be forced; it would be unwise to try even if it is for their best interest. For a person to act wisely, words must not only be heard, but also felt.

DARK LIGHT

LXXVI

A lot of people seem to be "trying" to do things. "Trying" to get better at something or trying to do something better. Eliminate try from your vocabulary. Just do it. Easier said than done right? Not really, because things are only as difficult as we perceive them to be. Change your perception of your task, and the task becomes easier.

DARK LIGHT

LXXVII

You must get to know yourself, on a deeper level, in order to know your purpose. Life becomes simpler when you understand yourself. In order to find the path outwardly, we must first journey on the path within.

DARK LIGHT

LXXVIII

We must be like water and adapt to any situation without losing our essence. Water can freeze to ice, can fill a cup, or become steam, but its core, never changes. We can adapt to any situation without changing who we are.

DARK LIGHT

LXXIX

Knowledge is not always wisdom. This is important to understand. There are many people in the world who are very knowledgeable but are certainly not wise. And there are also people who are not very educated in the traditional sense but are very wise. Knowledge has its place, but wisdom will and can go any and everywhere.

DARK LIGHT

LXXX

It is simpler to be wise for others than it is to apply that wisdom for ourselves. Don't just teach other people; make sure you are implementing those ways in your own life. Examine what you are and are not doing to improve yourself. Then ask yourself why aren't you doing it? Introspection is key to success. Question, examine, accept and change.

DARK LIGHT

LXXXI

Go for all that you want to go for without reservation. It's one thing to fail having gone for it all but another thing to fail because you held YOURSELF back. Sometimes our greatest hurdles are ourselves.

DARK LIGHT

LXXXII

No matter how big the obstacle seems, your relentless persistence will eventually keep going, and never lose sight of your goals. Life rewards the diligent, the strong, the smart, the wise, but mostly, the Persistent.

Love light and peace!

DARK LIGHT

LXXXIII

Everybody has "haters" in their life. Yes, those people who talk about you for no reason. Those who say they wish you success but secretly are envious and want you to fail. We all have them. That's their job! Your job is to keep living a life that's worthy of being hated on! When the haters stop hating on you, they've either got their self together, or you are slipping.

DARK LIGHT

LXXXIV

Sure there are a lot of things you want in life, and you want a lot of things to change, but in all honesty, Things could be Worse. Be grateful for each and every person and thing you have in your life. Although there may be a lot of people with more, there are many more people with less.

DARK LIGHT

LXXXV

Sometimes people are afraid of growing because the people we're around don't want to grow the way you're growing. Staying with people who don't want to grow will be like holding onto a rose while it's growing thorns; appreciate the beauty and time you had with it but learn to let it go.

DARK LIGHT

LXXXVI

Just because you are doing something you don't want to do now, doesn't mean it won't lead you to where you want to go later. Keep your mind open to new opportunities and focused on where you want to go. All roads don't lead to the same place, but that doesn't mean there's only one road to that place.

DARK LIGHT

LXXXVII

There may be many perceived obstacles that cross your path, if so, be like the Ant. Nothing ever stops it regardless of the obstacle. They walk over it or around it, but they never turn around.

DARK LIGHT

LXXXVIII

Understand that the things that you want, involve you getting out of your comfort zone. Just because you don't like a situation, or you're not happy with it, doesn't mean you're not comfortable with it. So until you're willing to get uncomfortable, to get comfortable, you'll never get what you truly want.

DARK LIGHT

LXXXIX

Social responsibility means helping others, not only helping those directly related to you. Although you may be on your grind to get yourself in a better situation, there are others that can only dream they were in the situation you're in. Receive graciously, give genuinely, learn incessantly and then teach lovingly.

DARK LIGHT

XC

Today think about what interests you. If you know what you like to do, find a way to make money doing it. Some of the happiest people I've met have turned their hobbies into something professional. In this moment, the only things that will stop you are the blocks YOU put up.

DARK LIGHT

XCI

We all must deal with trials and tribulations, problems and stress. Something different to think about today is; how do you deal with success? Think about it, we're all taught different ways to deal with failure, but maybe if we learn ways to deal with success, we'll attract more of it.

DARK LIGHT

XCII

Do not dwell in the past. Learn from it, let it go and move forward. It may be hard, but your life will be harder trying to hold on to what's already gone.

DARK LIGHT

There is no need to look outside of ourselves for any wisdom or guidance because all we need comes from within. In this day, realize that the light within you has the strength and the wisdom to get you through each and every day. Education can be expensive but it's not as high as the price of stupidity.

DARK LIGHT

Without imagination you may have all the knowledge to build, but you'll lack the ability to create. But with imagination, you may lack certain knowledge, but you'll still be able to thrive because your creativity will give you knowledge that you never knew you had. Think creatively, intuitively, and wisely.

DARK LIGHT

You can choose to live your life with integrity, and honesty, even if other people choose to live differently. People say, "Well I don't follow the 'Golden Rule' because other people don't do the same." Well, why should someone else's behavior and moral standard affect your own? I mean wouldn't you want more people in the world who are like that? The first way to incite change is to start with yourself.

DARK LIGHT

XCVI

We can only become what we believe we are capable of. Your potential is limitless, but only if you believe it to be. We often put the anchor down on our own ship. Ships, just like people, aren't meant to stay at the bay and be safe! Sail!

DARK LIGHT

XCVII

Failure is something that we all experience; it is a part of life. Failure can be a catalyst for progress, or regress, depending on how you look at it. See the good in every situation where you fail and move forward. This will lead to success, and even if it doesn't, it will certainly lead to peace.

DARK LIGHT

XCVIII

It's a new day, to get your life where you want it to go. It is in your control, but whether you choose to take control or not, is completely up to you. Things happen, but you can choose to be the cause, not the effect. Happiness in and of itself is a choice. It is only our thinking, not our circumstances, that will determine whether we will be happy or not.

DARK LIGHT

XCIX

The reason why life can be stressful is because we often go into things thinking about the outcome. Questions pop up in our mind like "will all this hard work, be worth it?" To escape those questions, we should pursue whatever we want, but with freedom from the attachment of results. Like water; just flow. Like the air; be open and like the trees; grow in the direction towards the light.

DARK LIGHT

C

Sometimes, people don't want to admit when they're wrong, but that doesn't mean you shouldn't hold them accountable when they are. Hold them accountable, and then let it go. Your ability to forgive shouldn't be determined by the person who committed the offense. Holding on to it, won't make it go away, nor will it make the situation any better. Move forward. At the end of it all, life won't be measured by your status and what you had, it will be about who you were and what you gave. What have you given?

DARK LIGHT

Never be afraid to start over, even if you've invested a lot of time energy and effort. If you created something you don't like, or no longer suits you, you can create something different.

Life is what you make it, but the question is what are you making? Putting down the shovel is the first step towards getting out of a hole and never picking it up again is the second. How you get out of the hole, is up to you, but without the first 2 steps, you will not get out.

DARK LIGHT

CII

It is easier to prevent a habit, then to break one. Discipline is key for both, but more is required to break a bad habit. Breaking a bad habit is like trying to put the brakes on a bike while riding down a mountain. Sure it can be done, but why go down the mountain in the first place? Discipline is knowing that you have the choice to go down, but not allowing yourself to go.

DARK LIGHT

It is your choice to do what you want with this moment, and it is your choice to choose what you learn from it. Choose wisely, and always acknowledge that you can choose your actions, but you cannot choose your consequences. Sometimes a day doesn't start off the way you would like it to, but we have the ability to change its course. If you want to have a great day, believe that you will, and it will happen. If you think and believe you'll have a bad day, you will. Now I'm not saying that you'll get all you want on a good day, but certainly it'll be better than what you would perceive a bad day to be. It is all in our control. So have a great day!

DARK LIGHT

CIV

As you find out where you want to go in life, you need to associate with like-minded people. They don't have to want the exact same things that you want, but the underlying themes should be similar. If success, love, and prosperity are the things that you want, then hanging around people who are not going towards that will stifle your progress. Life is hard enough, but your friends shouldn't be obstacles too.

DARK LIGHT

CV

If you make your needs into your wants, then I suppose you won't have to worry about wanting what you don't need. Seeing is not just something that is done physically but it is also done perceptively, intellectually, and philosophically. Do not be closed minded in your thinking so much so that you will not see where someone else may be coming from. Sometimes when you change your perception, you'll realize that there is a lot more to be seen.

DARK LIGHT

CVI

Sometimes you need to do and not think and other times you need to think and not do. Wisdom is, knowing when to do which. When asked to do something out of a person's comfort zone, it seems that a lot of people say, "I'm not that type of person" or I can't do things like that. You are who you create yourself to be. You define yourself. So all you have to do is just do those things that you weren't doing before. Then you would become the person you thought you weren't before. Don't think, just do it.

DARK LIGHT

CVII

Do not be concerned with comparing your life to other people's perceived life. Your time for success will come if you keep doing what you're supposed to do and believing in yourself. Success comes to those who are dedicated, diligent and determined. Its not a race, there's no rush, even though you want it sooner rather than later. Patience, and persistence will get you where you want to go or get you where you're supposed to be.

DARK LIGHT

CVIII

You only get one chance, to make a first impression. How do you carry yourself? You can say, "I am smart" or "I am talented" or "I am confident" but if the way you walk and carry yourself doesn't correspond, it is only words. Think about what message are you sending with your actions, they hold more weight than anything else. If there is a dissonance between how you see yourself, and who you want to be, figure out why, accept it, and then change when necessary. You have the power, now all you need to do is use it.

DARK LIGHT

When dealing with a difficult situation, getting through it and learning from it is more educational than just running from it and then looking back. Take the time to think what you did to get in the situation. If you run from it without thinking about how you got yourself into it, how will you know how to avoid getting back into a similar situation? Do what you have to do now so you can do what you want later.

DARK LIGHT

CX

If you feel like you're always attracting and getting into a relationship with the wrong guy/girl, you have to start questioning yourself and what you are really attracted to. Sometimes you have to look inward to find out what's happening outward. How willing are you to seek the truth? Certainly it can be freeing but it can also be painful because you can't go back to living the same way. It's the death of the old you to be reborn to live in the light of the truth. It can hurt to know the truth, that's why people avoid asking questions that lead them there. The question then is: "are you willing to die in order to live?"

DARK LIGHT

CXI

If you have been doing great, feeling great and your friends aren't happy for you then you need to start looking for new friends. If your friends are only there for you when you're down, what does that say about them? Or if you're only there for them when they're down, what does that say about you? The ability to be happy for someone even when you're not happy marks the essence of a true friend.

.

DARK LIGHT

CXII

Simple thoughts; complain less, appreciate more, talk less, listen more, fear less, hope more, argue less, love more, worry less, relax more, doubt less, believe more, work less, and play more. It is better to not speak but do a lot, than to speak a lot and do noth ing.

The best leaders know how to follow. In our lives we need to be both leaders and followers. You must be strong, humble, and willing to be either. On a deeper note, you need to follow your intuition, which will put you in a position to be followed. How well do you follow yourself and how well do you allow yourself to lead?

DARK LIGHT

If you want to be successful, be prepared for the responsibility that comes with it. You will not get to where you want to go without the people in your life that supported you. Don't forget about those people, or the people who are trying to get where you are. We become, so that others can become.

In order to communicate a message effectively, you must be a good listener. Anyone can say words, but if you don't listen then you won't know what words need to be said. Seek to understand, then to be understood.

DARK LIGHT

CXIV

Birth and death are things that we all will experience in our life. Those 2 experiences are mandatory. But how you fill the life in between is entirely up to you. What will your life be about? If you keep doing what you're doing, you'll keep getting what you're getting. No need to be surprised by the results!

.

DARK LIGHT

CXV

The reason why it is hard to be a good teacher is because you must live your teachings. The "Do as I say not as I do" does not apply when trying to convince others. The best teachers, speak less, and say more, preach less and act more. We all are teachers, the question is then, what exactly are you teaching, and have you learned the lesson?

.

DARK LIGHT
CXVI

Never forget the gift of your own intuition. It is something we all have. It is that little voice that will never yell, but if listened to, will always steer you in the right direction.

Everybody has to start somewhere. Even if you consider it to be nowhere in terms of your progress, it's still further than if you did not start at all. So what ever you have been meaning to do, whatever you have been putting off, get started. What are you waiting for anyway? No one else will do it for you.

.

DARK LIGHT

CXVII

It's not always easy. Life doesn't always give you what we want, but it is in this where you find your strength.

DARK LIGHT

CXVIII

In life, sometimes the tests come before the lessons; so don't go into things thinking, "I don't want to fail". Go into things just doing the best that you can, because it's not really about passing or failing, its about what you learn from it.

DARK LIGHT

CIX

Never take your health for granted. To eat some things in moderation is one thing, but to constantly put junk in your body because "it tastes good" ask yourself this: Are you Eating to Live, or Living to Eat?

.

.

DARK LIGHT

CXX

God, Karma, or whatever label you would like to put on it, takes care of people and situations much better than we ever can. Let go and move on.

.

DARK LIGHT

CXXI

If the environment you are currently in, functions as something negative for you, removing yourself may be only a small part of the battle. If you do not change yourself, then you might be prone to recreating the same negative environment you were in originally. But if you change on the inside, the environment will change based on your changed perspective, removing the bad, and including the good, or removing the perceptions of bad and good altogether.

DARK LIGHT

CXXII

Each day, your life will bring, what you give your attention to.

.

DARK LIGHT

CXXIII

The only thing that will get you to where you want to go is persistence. If you constantly try different things, and give up on it too soon, it will be like running on a treadmill. Sure, you'll get a workout, but at the end of it all, you will have gotten nowhere with anything.

DARK LIGHT

CXXIV

Why has the idea of having a conscience become a thing of the past? The "golden rule" does not have to be obsolete, but if you do not follow it, don't expect others to follow it for you. Some may not follow it anyway, but karma is a funny thing. Spread light and love and you will receive light and love. Spread bad things and you will, receive worse!

DARK LIGHT

CXXV

At the end of the day, reflect on what you've done, think about what you need to do, and then carry out a plan to get it done.

DARK LIGHT

CXXVI

Learning from your mistakes, is a hard lesson, but it is a harder lesson to learn, when you're not honest with the mistake you've made. Admitting to yourself the 'wrongs' and the 'rights' about how you handled a situation is the first step towards learning from it. You cannot change what you don't acknowledge. Be honest with yourself! Otherwise, repeating it will be the next step.

DARK LIGHT

CXXVII

Change your thoughts and you will change your life. Your life is only a manifestation of past thoughts. Thoughts play not just an important role in what you want for your life, honestly, it's the only role that matters. Your actions are only manifested thoughts. So if you want to change your current situation, change your thoughts.

.

DARK LIGHT
CXXVIII

Be more concerned with what you ARE, rather than what you DO.

.

DARK LIGHT

CXXIX

Experience teaches more than books, but that doesn't mean you shouldn't read.

DARK LIGHT

CXXX

On interviews, it shouldn't be just the interviewer asking you questions, and you just answering. What will set you apart from people they are interviewing? Create a conversation and dialogue. Challenge them! Ask them questions about their career the pros AND the cons of the position and how they got there. Then, when they think about the interview, they had with you they'll remember the conversation, and that, will set you apart.

DARK LIGHT

CXXXI

Knowledge is only power if you are using it in a way to benefit yourself. There seem to be a lot of people that "know" things but tend not to do what they know. Better to be a person that knows a little, but does what they know, rather than a person who knows a lot, but does very little.

DARK LIGHT

CXXXII

The little things in life can be as simple and as small as saying a kind word to a person, being there for a friend, or having a friend to be there for you. Never forget that we are all interconnected in the human experience. Spread love, light, and you will receive it in return.

DARK LIGHT

CXXXIII

Sometimes you learn more things when there is no teacher to teach you the thing you need to learn. Solely relying on traditional education only will limit your knowledge to just traditional ways of thinking. You can expand and grow much more when people intend to teach themselves something. Learn about different things and expand in ways that traditional education would leave out.

DARK LIGHT

CXXXIV

The fear of failing should never be greater than happiness in succeeding. The greatest failure is when you don't even make the attempt.

DARK LIGHT

CXXXV

A lot of people complain about situations or complain about things they can change. If it is changeable, change it. Yes, it will require work, but if the work is worth it then either do it, or don't do it. It's just that simple. Complaining is wasted energy, and energy is limited. Instead of complaining you could be using that energy to move forward.

DARK LIGHT

CXXXVI

Say what you mean and mean what you say. Never be afraid to say something that's the truth. If you choose to speak, make sure your words, are worth more than your silence. To lead an orchestra one must turn its back to the audience.

DARK LIGHT

CXXXVII

Age is only what YOU say it is...if you say, "I'm old" then you are. If you say, "I'm young" then that is true as well. Like fine wine you can get better with time ;)

DARK LIGHT

CXXXVIII

You don't have to be loud to get your point across. Volume does not always increase the effectiveness of communication. Sometimes silence, is even more effective, and louder than yelling.

DARK LIGHT

CXXXIX

Live one day at a time, enjoying one moment at a time, and accept hardship as a pathway to peace. Do what you can; let go of what you can't.

DARK LIGHT
CXL

To hear the truth is hard, but to act on it is harder. Even though it is hard, it is necessary for personal growth. Do what you have to do now, so you can do what you want later.

DARK LIGHT

CXLI

Knowledge is a responsibility. It is not something that you can just acquire without the expectation of action to follow. You can't use ignorance as an excuse anymore, because now, you KNOW better.

DARK LIGHT

CXLII

Understand that traditional education should not be the only way you seek education. Traditional education alone should only get you to want to know more about what's not being taught, and what's not being said. Truth, especially on the subject of history, is always told to the masses from the eyes of the winner.

DARK LIGHT

CXLIII

Sometimes, it's often ourselves that serves as a roadblock in getting where we want. Self-sabotage is prevalent in our world. Take a careful examination at what you're doing, and why you're doing. Procrastination is also a self-sabotaging mechanism.

DARK LIGHT

CXLIV

Someone else's situation may appear better, but you don't know what else is going on with them that may be worse than you. Never envy anyone, because you block your own blessings by not being grateful for what you have. Spread love and light, and you will receive love and light. Spread negative emotions and that is what you will continue to attract for yourself. In life, you get what you focus on.

DARK LIGHT

CXLV

You are going through life's day-to-day activities, but are you thinking? Are you stopping to examine the things that you are doing in your life and understanding the direction it may take you in? This IS more important than the destination or the journey because those are only manifestations of thoughts and actions. But without thinking about the steps you are taking, where are you really going?

DARK LIGHT

CXLVI

The measure of success should never be apart of willingness to be indifferent to the suffering of other people. Although we are different, we must understand that we are all a part of nature, the environment, the ecosystem, and the human connection.

DARK LIGHT

All things must come to an end. This can be good or bad, but mainly it is the continued cycle and process of life. Each new beginning represents an end, and each end represents a beginning. Know that whether the change is good or bad, it will not last forever. Make the most out of the good change and learn the lessons out of the bad. All things will not last forever.

DARK LIGHT

CXLVIII

A life unexamined is a life wasted. Introspection is a key element in a successful and happy life. Let your inward change your outward, not your outward changing your inward. Be the Cause, not the Effect. Life will have its bumps, but perception will determine how bumpy it is.

DARK LIGHT

CXLIX

Sometimes, people tend to just go through the motions. This is merely existing, but not living. With every event, situation, or circumstance something can be learned from it. If you're doing something and feel you're getting nothing out of it, Look harder, search deeper. If you still find nothing, why are you doing it in the first place?

DARK LIGHT
CL

All you can do, all you need to do, is give it your all, whatever that IT is for you. Make sure while in the process of going for what you want, you are doing everything you can do and giving it your best. People are afraid to do this because of the fear of failure, but it is worse not to try than to try and not succeed. Life is about trying, failing or succeeding and then trying again.

DARK LIGHT

CLI

If life is like art, then be the master of your own creation. Matter fact, you already are, the question is, what are You creating? Whether things are going well for you or not, remember, you are the artist of this masterpiece. Create something you will love, and it will be so. Create something you don't, and it will be so as well. The greatest thing about being the artist is, you can always create another picture.

DARK LIGHT

CLII

You can tell more about a person by what they say about other people rather than what people say about them.

DARK LIGHT

CLIII

Sure you may have learned things through experience, school, and books but that isn't even 1 percent of what's out in the world. We must continually challenge ourselves to grow spiritually, intellectually, emotionally, philosophically, and critically. If not, then you are wasting your potential. You must seek this info; it will not be taught to you. Live, learn and grow.

DARK LIGHT

CLIV

People feel that we all are so different, which can be true in ways, but we are all a part of the human connection. Therefore we need not to be judgmental on your neighbor even if they do things that are different from what you do. Seek to understand, then to be understood. We all are in a similar boat, even when it doesn't appear that way. Spread love and light to all and you will receive love and light in return.

DARK LIGHT

CLV

Continue to stay focused on what you want. You have the power and control to go after and achieve anything you want in this life. The only limitations you have are the ones you put on yourself. Even if you feel you should have started pursuing what you wanted earlier, it's not too late. Remember, it's never too late to BE what you could have been.

DARK LIGHT
CLVI

People look for quotes and advice, but when you find it do you take it? Do you look at it and say, wow, that cheered me up/or made me feel good for the moment, but then don't apply it? If so, then what's the point of seeking it? We should seek to grow spiritually, intellectually, and emotionally each and every day. If good advice or wise words are shared for a moment, then they can be applied for a lifetime.

DARK LIGHT

CLVII

Be true to you. However that may be, however it may come across, be true to you. People often know this but don't follow it enough, so today here's a reminder. "To thine own self be true." Everybody has intuition; it is our mind that tries to "logic" it in a way that goes against our natural intuitiveness. Your intuition will not lead you wrong, but you can't be afraid of the direction it may take you in.

DARK LIGHT

CLVIII

What's the difference between a flower that gets all sun and a flower that gets all rain? The answer is nothing because they both die earlier than they should. I say this because rain in your life serves as much of a purpose as the sun. It is just how we view it that may be a problem. The flower opens up for the sun and the rain, knowing it needs both. How we view things will be how we get **(or not get)** through things.

DARK LIGHT

CLIX

A lot of people think they know themselves, but if you're not taking a deeper look at why you're doing the things you do, then you don't know yourself as well as you think. It takes courage to look within at the good and the bad and make a conscious effort to change. Life and all its ups and downs is not the hardest journey. The hardest journey is the journey from within.

DARK LIGHT

CLX

Discipline is not only an integral part of life, but it is truly one of the few ways to accomplish what you want and have a satisfying fulfilling life. No one said it was going to be easy, especially when others around aren't moving forward with courage. You must be strong and fight temptation, whatever that is for you. You can do it! The sun's strength comes from within, and so must yours.

DARK LIGHT

CLXI

Think like an entrepreneur. Think about what you love to do, then find a way to make $ doing it. I'm asking you think creatively today. And just think, the person who owns the company that you work for, that's what they did. They own their labor, and your labor. Why not work to own yours?

DARK LIGHT

CLXII

Whatever you do, whatever goals you set for yourself, Begin with the End in mind. While you're working towards it, you'll encounter some things that you might not enjoy doing but if it's leading you to the place you want to be, then keep going. Keep that end product in your mind as you continue your journey. Focus on the desired outcome, not the circumstances that you face while heading towards your destination.

Love light and peace!

DARK LIGHT

CLXIII

I know a lot of people that want to be successful, some who want to be great, and very few who want to be wise. The person who seeks out wisdom will be able to navigate through life smoother, because of the foundation of knowledge that they have built. No one really talks about being wise anymore, but how many decisions in your life have been made that were unwise? People say. "Why talk about wisdom?" well, why not?

DARK LIGHT

CLXIV

If you're thinking of what to say while someone else is speaking, you're not listening. You may be hearing the words, but you're not listening on level that will allow for complete understanding. Silence is very important part of a conversation. When we communicate with one another, seek to understand, then to be understood. If those 2 things aren't the goals, then why talk at all? To hear yourself??

DARK LIGHT

CLXV

You can continually say things to try to help others but the responsibility in that is that we must live our teachings. Without that, the message you're giving is one of contradiction. Bear the responsibility of improving yourself, and others will follow more than just the words of your advice. Are you practicing what you preach?

DARK LIGHT

CLXVI

You can do better; you can be better, but only if you are willing to change. Sometimes we become so stuck in our same pattern of thinking that it stifles our growth. Sure there may be a few principles that you stick by, but if there is evidence suggesting that change is needed, then you must do so in order to grow.

DARK LIGHT

CLXVII

Speak true to your heart, regardless of if it hurts someone else. Try to be mindful of how you're saying it, but be honest, and understand there may be consequences for your honesty. Some say it's easier to lie, but it puts a stain on your integrity and your morale. At the end of it all, the worse person to lie to is YOU.

DARK LIGHT

CLXVIII

Sometimes we look outside and think, "man this weather sucks, its raining" But rain is just as much necessary as the sun. It is both that take part in cultivating life on earth. Each of us has our own periods of "Rain" in our life, and this as well, it is necessary for growth. How we view the rain, will determine how much we will grow from it.

DARK LIGHT

CLXIX

It takes courage to try and if the first attempt doesn't work then try again. You'll never reach your potential if you're too afraid of making mistakes while trying to reach it.

DARK LIGHT

CLXX

Your goals should aim to find something in life that you look forward to doing, and when you are finished for the day, you are proud to say you have done.

DARK LIGHT

CLXXI

Life is about the cycle of living and dying. When you decide to put down certain assumptions, in order to be educated and live more deeply and fully, that in itself is a death. It is the death of your old self, and the rebirth of your new self that is more knowledgeable and educated. This cycle continues for the rest of your life. Grow and have the courage to die, so you may grow again.

DARK LIGHT

CLXXII

Only people that have woken up can make their dreams come true. I hope you wake up today and realize the sky isn't the limit, your mind is.

DARK LIGHT

CLXXIII

Don't be afraid to be different. Whether its what you think or how you dress or what you listen to, never be afraid of that, even if it's in the company of others who might not accept you for who you are. If they can't accept you, change the company! For every few that don't accept you there will be many more that will. Remember." To thine own self, be true." Have a great day!

DARK LIGHT

CLXXIV

We become what we think. Who we are and who we become is only a manifestation of our thoughts. So before you think about how much of life you can't control, think about that. Control what you can; let go of what you can't.

DARK LIGHT

CLXXV

Faith is such an important part of life, yet so many of us lack and waiver in having it. I'm not talking about some nice sounding optimism and quote that lack substance. I'm talking about believing and hoping in things and ideas even when you do not have absolute evidence leading to your conclusion. Sometimes we just have to take that step, even if we don't know where the staircase will lead.

DARK LIGHT

CLXXVI

When getting advice from anyone, even if they are older, it does not mean they necessarily have the best advice. Some people when getting older are like fine wine getting better with time. And others are like Bananas, the older they get the more visibly rotten they become. As you get older, think about the person you WANT to be and the person you WILL be if you keep the same mentality.

DARK LIGHT

CLXXVII

Pay close attention to your thoughts today. You get what you focus on. We can only change and improve our circumstance by first changing our thoughts. How much more improved would your life be if you changed your mindset? All those people that are and were deemed to be successful and great became that because of the belief to act on their thoughts.

DARK LIGHT

CLXXVIII

Aspire to be great, not just successful. Being great means that your purpose is bigger than yourself. It means that it is connected to something that is more than just you. To be great, is deeper, more profound than being successful. Being great doesn't necessarily equate to success, but it does mean that in some way, you have touched the life of someone else. Greatness lies in all of us, have the courage to act.

DARK LIGHT

CLXXIX

Take some time today to really decide what you want, and more importantly what is the price that you are willing to pay for it? If there is too much that you are unwilling to sacrifice, then you don't really want it as bad as you say you do! Be honest with yourself!

DARK LIGHT

CLXXX

The only difference between people that become successful and the people that don't is that the successful people have an unwavering inner-belief, and they take action with that belief in mind. GO FOR "IT". Whatever that "IT" is for you.

DARK LIGHT

CLXXXI

We all have made mistakes, but in order to truly learn from it we need to forgive ourselves of that mistake. To forgive yourself doesn't mean you'll forget what you did, but it does mean that you don't have to live there and stay in that past reality. Learn to let go.

DARK LIGHT

CLXXXII

Think about the way you see "reality" today, for it is all an illusion that we create with our mind. What's your reality?

DARK LIGHT

CLXXXIII

Do not get impatient with yourself because what you want isn't manifesting quick enough. Life and attainment of goals is about the journey, not the destination.

DARK LIGHT

CLXXXIV

Happiness is a choice. It is not based on circumstance; otherwise it can be easily taken away from you. Happiness is something that is internal, that almost no situation can take away from you. So today make the conscious decision, to be happy.

Thoughts for today.

Me:" Good morning!"

Other person:" What's good about it?"

Me: You woke up! There are a lot of people that didn't!"

DARK LIGHT

CLXXXV

I have often times seen people become very upset when they hold the door for a person, and they didn't say thank you. Now I'm not saying I don't understand but if you get that upset, why did you do it in the first place? Hopefully to not get something in return. Check your intentions. Do to DO don't DO to Get.

DARK LIGHT

CLXXXVI

Leaders need to follow sometimes, and followers need to lead sometimes. To get the most out of each situation and circumstance we encounter, we must be willing to play both roles.

DARK LIGHT

CLXXXVII

It shouldn't always take for others to say, "you shouldn't do this" or "you shouldn't eat that" for you not to do it. You know what is right and wrong for you so why continue to do it? Because it feels good? Is that a good enough reason? Usually it isn't.

DARK LIGHT

CLXXXVIII

Who do you want to be, and are you acting like the person that you say you are? Ask yourself these questions today.

DARK LIGHT

CLXXXIX

In order to get what you really want in life; you must use your creativity and imagination to get it.

DARK LIGHT

CXC

The ability to have a great reputation is in all of us, but it requires action that is congruent with whom we want to appear to be. You can't just want a good reputation, but never act in the way that would show it.

DARK LIGHT

CXCI

Sometimes life is about being disciplined; therefore you can't always do what we want when we want to. You must do what you have to do now, so you can do what you want later.

DARK LIGHT

CXCII

What happens when you can't find the opportunities you are looking for in life? You create them.

DARK LIGHT

CXCIII

Your situation is not permanent, but how you handle it will have lasting effects.

DARK LIGHT

CXCIV

Only those who dare to go to far will be the
ones who will truly know how far they can go.

DARK LIGHT

CXCV

One of the hardest lessons in life is learning to listen to yourself. Intuition will not lead you astray or misguide you. The tricky part is to know the difference between intuition and what is a thought that is more emotionally based.

DARK LIGHT

CXCVI

People may be ready FOR change, but unless they are ready TO change there will be NO change.

DARK LIGHT

CXCVII

Sometimes you must learn to appreciate presence, through absence. We often times take for granted people that are around us and who we think will always be there. Take this time today thank someone who is close to you, who you always want to be there.

DARK LIGHT

CXCVIII

Do not run from a situation that is uncomfortable. There is a way you can deal with it and overcome. Remember, fortune favors the brave.

DARK LIGHT

CXCIX

Go in it, with the end in mind. If you always keep yourself focused on the goal, it's easier to do the things in order to get there, even if they are things you don't like.

DARK LIGHT

CC

Readiness for something, whatever it is, is shown and not told. Show readiness through action without words, rather than words without actions.

DARK LIGHT

CCI

Success is not a matter of chance; it's a matter of choice. It is not something that comes to the lucky but is a result of the diligent and the courageous.

DARK LIGHT

CCII

Wanting something to happen and believing it will are two different things. You can want something to happen but if you don't believe it will happen, it won't happen.

DARK LIGHT

CCIII

We as people should never cease pursuit of the truth, no matter what area of life it is in. We must keep questioning, because if you are not inquisitive, lies become believable truths.

DARK LIGHT

CCIV

Make sure that although you have a lot on your own plate you are still kind to those around us. Everybody is going through something, even if it looks like they aren't.

DARK LIGHT

CCV

Each day you live is one day closer to the day you will die. What does your life mean? Are you helping others, or leading a life that will only help you? We cannot change our birth, or our death, but what we fill in between is your choice. What choices will you make?

DARK LIGHT

CCVI

There are many different ways of looking at the same picture. Those who can alter their perceptions can alter their lives to their advantage.

DARK LIGHT

CCVII

Start examining what it is that you really want out of life. Then understand why you are not where you said you'd like to be.

DARK LIGHT

CCVIII

Fear is perpetuated all on the premise of ignorance. Choose to allow education to influence your thoughts, words, and actions and not assumptions or mass media. Allow your experience to be the catalyst for your thoughts and beliefs.

DARK LIGHT

CCIX

Make sure you take the time to work on yourself, even if it's only in small steps. It will ALWAYS be to your benefit.

DARK LIGHT

CCX

Happiness comes from within, something that cannot be taken away or given. Things may add or subtract from that but, at its core, being happy can only come from you.

DARK LIGHT

CCXI

You shouldn't do to get; you should just do to Do. So if you're doing a good deed for someone, only because of what you might get in return, then you probably shouldn't be doing it at all.

DARK LIGHT

CCXII

If you have an idea about something you want to do, act now, with one small step at a time and keep moving forward towards the light.

DARK LIGHT

CCXIII

Attitude can be contagious, is yours worth catching? Exude positive energy that you would also like to receive. Energy can be like a boomerang, so if it's going to eventually come back to you, you should put out something good.

DARK LIGHT

CCXIV

So today let's make sure you are being grateful for what you have. If you want more in the future, how can you receive it if you are not grateful for what we have in the present?

DARK LIGHT

CCXV

Don't doubt your own ability to overcome, any situation. If you believe and know you can get through it, you will.

DARK LIGHT

CCXVI

Acknowledge and understand that sometimes, your biggest obstacle in your life is You. Believe in yourself and pursue what you want with all your heart, and the rest will follow.

DARK LIGHT

CCXVII

Today, think about how you can be more action oriented. If you have said you can do something, then why haven't you done it yet? Don't think of the excuses as to why you haven't, just do it. Use fewer words and use more action.

DARK LIGHT

CCXVIII

If you are talking with someone and seeing
that no logical sense is going to penetrate their
brain, let it go. You can't force knowledge on to
anyone in the same way you can't fill a cup
that's already full.

DARK LIGHT

The sky shouldn't be your limit, if so then your vision is limited. Embracing this philosophy might suggest that you feel you are only able to achieve what you can physically see. So if it's not visible physically, does this mean it's impossible? Limited goals will lead to limited results.

DARK LIGHT

CCXX

Today, think about watching your words and how you say things. Sometimes we speak and the true intention of our words is lost because of how we said it, even if the intention is benevolent.

DARK LIGHT

CCXXI

Although I am not anti-traditional education, I will say this: school does not teach you about yourself. Therefore those who are invested in only traditional schooling (example: college) will miss out on the lessons that people who diversify their education will learn. Remember this: degrees don't=wisdom, they=knowledge but if you don't know yourself; what do you really know, and how can you truly know anyone else?

DARK LIGHT

CCXXII

If you want to see nicer people in the world, be a nicer person. If you wish to see more kindness in the world, be a kinder person. Examine yourself before you critique and remember the opposite of courageous is not cowardice, but conformity and indifference.

DARK LIGHT

CCXXIII

The successful people in life are go-getters, either you are getting what you want, or you're watching someone else get what you could have gotten. Which one will you be?

.

DARK LIGHT

CCXXIV

Take a notice of ants today. When you put your foot in its way, it moves around you, takes a different direction or sometimes just walks over you, but it never stops moving to where it wants to go. Never stop going, no matter what's in front of you.

DARK LIGHT

CCXXV

What do you do when you know what to do, but you don't feel like doing what you know? You ACT into it. Act as if you want to do it, then your emotion and energy will follow through and you will transform yourself into wanting to do it. Simply put, when you don't feel like doing what's necessary, act as if you want to and then do it!

DARK LIGHT

CCXXVI

So today, make sure you're doing everything you need to do to reach the level of success you want. If you're not, ask yourself why, and if you already know, then take action!

DARK LIGHT

CCXXVII

When you have a goal in mind, things or people try to come in your way to block you from getting where we want to go. The only thing will get you to your goal is being persistent in going after them. Anything worth it won't be easy.

DARK LIGHT

CCXXVIII

Take time out today, even if for just a moment, to see or vision what you want. Then, take a step towards it, even if it is small.

DARK LIGHT

Never confuse motion with action. A person may not be moving around a lot but accomplishing much. And vice versa a person could be moving around a lot and still doing nothing!

DARK LIGHT

CCXXX

Instead of thinking, "I just want to get through the day", start thinking, "I am going to create the day!"

DARK LIGHT

CCXXXI

The way to happiness is not attaching your happiness to anyone or anything. Be happy not because everything you desire manifests, but because you don't attach your happiness to everything manifesting.

DARK LIGHT
ACKNOWLEDGMENTS

To my wonderful mother, Diane Robinson, who taught me that persistence is everything, and who helped instill in me, that we are here to be ourselves. Thank you mom.

To my father, George Robinson Jr., who always encouraged me and made me laugh in difficult times. To my sister, Jennifer Fass, whom I am grateful to have grown up with by my side, I am grateful that you are my sister.

To my mentor and friend Cordell Grooms who saw the value in what I was writing about and encouraged me to publish. Thank you for supporting me through this process.

To my professor, Dr. Jermaine Archer, who

DARK LIGHT

gave me the simple yet profound advice, "to just write", I appreciate your wisdom. To Ann Hinds, you showed me what it looks like to walk with grace. Thank you for being you.

To my wonderful partner Victoria DaCosta, your love and support has been unrelenting through this journey. I am so thankful that you are my partner.

And to my best friend, Melissa Hinds-Robinson, who taught me the value of seeking my own Light by going within. I honor and salute you my friend. To my ancestors, for without you all I would not be here and able to stand tall. It is because of your Light and Love that I have had the courage of going into the Dark. This is for all of you.

DARK LIGHT

DARK LIGHT
ABOUT THE AUTHOR

seven is a student of life and becoming a master of herself. seven has lived her life exploring, learning, and allowing life, along with her intuition to be her greatest teacher. She grew up in Long Island, NY where she eventually got two degrees in undergrad, and then she moved on to getting her Master's at UMASS Boston. She realized as she continued to grow that the truest knowledge was not found in classrooms or books but only within. Since her departure from traditional education, she has lived a life, where she

DARK LIGHT

teaches people how to be more in touch with themselves. She is adamant that she does not see herself as a coach, but instead as a facilitator of internal dialogue. seven has worked with people from various ages and various backgrounds with the purposeful intention of helping people to find their Light by leading them lovingly through the Dark.

EMAIL

pamela.robinson24@gmail.com

INSTAGRAM

dark_light_7777777

DARK LIGHT

www.ingramcontent.com/pod-product-compliance
Lightning Source LLC
Chambersburg PA
CBHW051819090426
42736CB00011B/1556